BOUNCING BACK

with Big Bird

A Book about Resilience

Jill Colella

Lerner Publications ◆ Minneapolis

Sesame Street's mission has always been about teaching kids much more than simply the ABCs and 123s. This series of books about nurturing the positive character traits of generosity, respect, empathy, positive thinking, resilience, and persistence will help children grow into the best versions of themselves. So come along with your funny, furry friends from Sesame Street as they learn about making themselves—and the world—smarter, stronger, and kinder.

—Sincerely, the Editors at Sesame Street

TABLE OF CONTENTS

What Is Resilience?

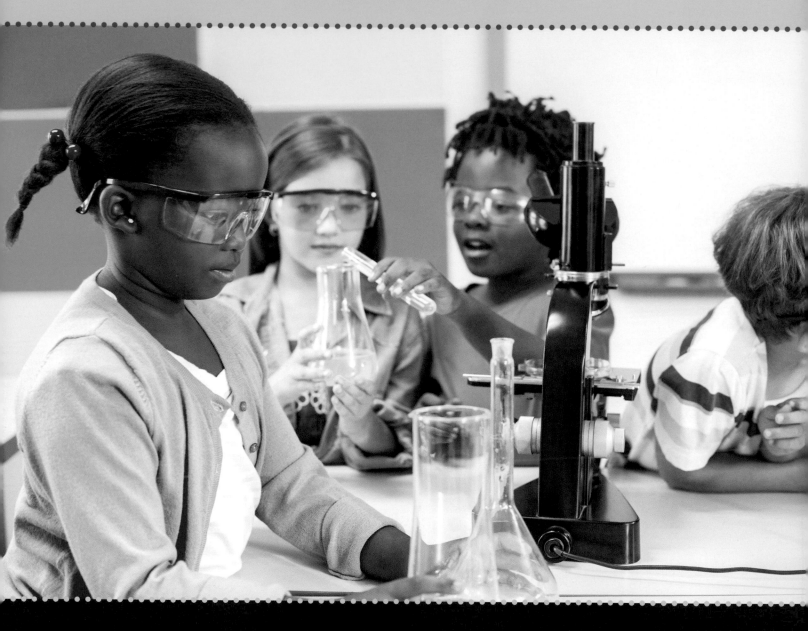

Resilience helps us get back up when we fall down.

Resilience means we keep going even when things are hard.

When something feels hard, you can bounce back.

When did you feel that something was scary or hard?

There are many ways to face a problem.

Everyone has big feelings. It's okay
to feel frustrated, sad, or afraid.

When I remember that other kids feel the same way, I don't feel alone.

Remember that feelings come and go. They are not permanent.

Take time to feel your feelings.
Then name and express them.

We can choose what to do
when we feel frustrated.

Who can you talk to about your feelings?

We can talk to people who love us.

Try to look at your problem in a new way.

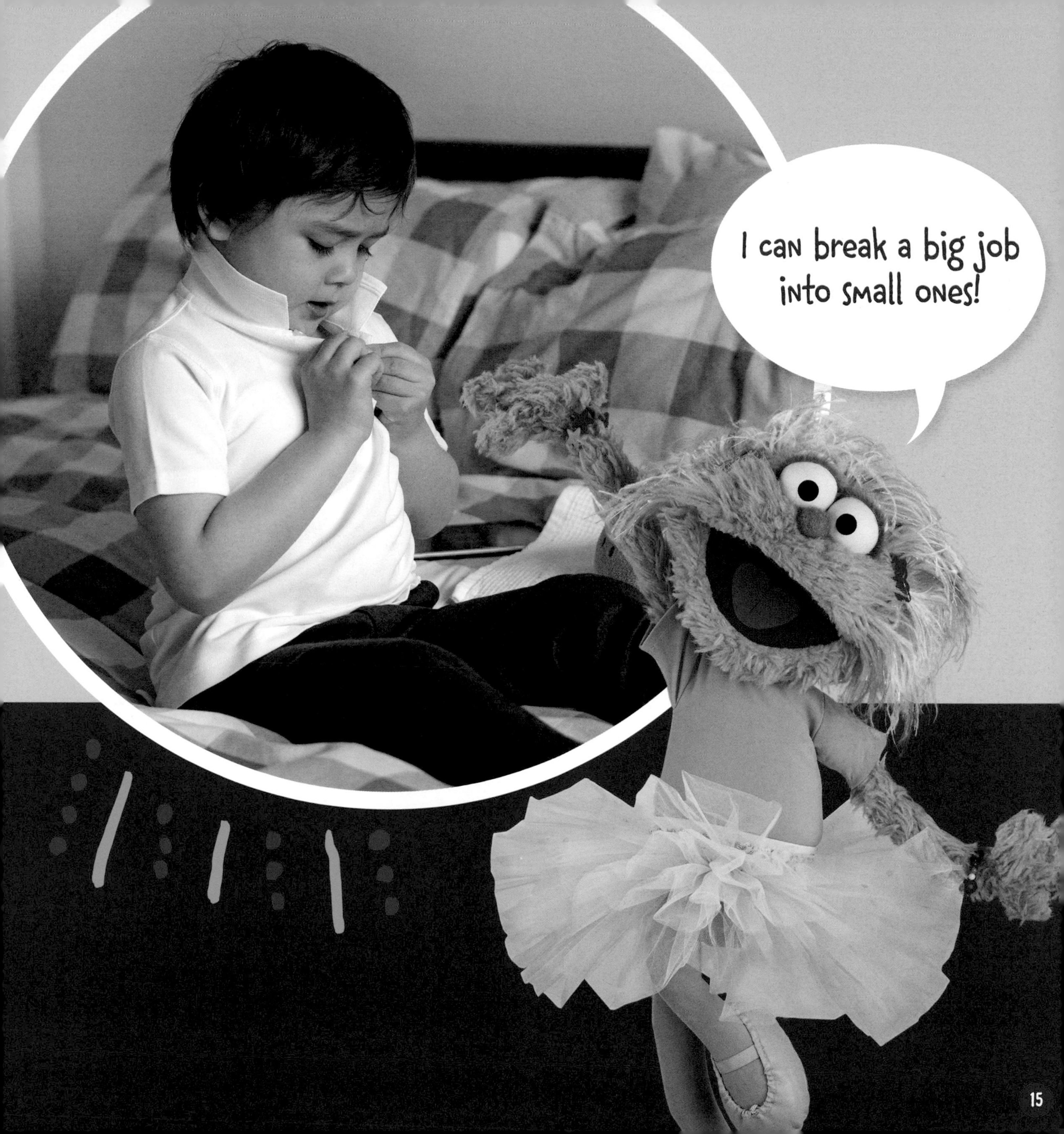
I can break a big job into small ones!

Be kind and patient with yourself.
Try taking a deep breath.

Can you think of
other ways to
treat yourself
with kindness?

When something seems hard, resilience helps us to keep trying.

I feel good
when I learn
a new song.

Our resilience helps us discover all the amazing things in the world.

Let's skate, paint, and make new friends!

BE A BUDDY!

Make a list of all the things that make you special. Keep this list, and read it when you feel like giving up. Then make a list for a friend. Use that list to help your friend be resilient too.

Glossary

amazing: surprising or good

discover: find out about

frustrated: upset or stuck

patient: calm and relaxed

permanent: lasting forever

Learn More

Bushman, Susanne M. *Don't Give Up.* Minneapolis: Jump!, 2020.

Colella, Jill. *Keep Trying with Abby: A Book about Persistence.* Minneapolis: Lerner Publications, 2021.

Olson, Elsie. *Be Strong! A Hero's Guide to Being Resilient.* Minneapolis: Super Sandcastle, 2020.

Index

Photo Acknowledgments

Additional image credits: wavebreakmedia/Shutterstock.com, p. 4; Double_H/Shutterstock.com, p. 5; A3pfamily/Shutterstock.com, p. 6; Motortion Films/Shutterstock.com, p. 7; Hung Chung Chih/Shutterstock.com, p. 8; tcareob72/Shutterstock.com, p. 9; PK Studio/Shutterstock.com, p. 10; Flamingo Images/Shutterstock.com, p. 11; Wanida_Sri/Shutterstock.com, p. 12; Lordn/Shutterstock.com, p. 13; Rawpixel.com/Shutterstock.com, pp. 14, 20; Ann in the uk/Shutterstock.com, p. 15; Ruslan Shugushev/Shutterstock.com, p. 16; Ronnachai Palas/Shutterstock.com, p. 17; FamVeld/Shutterstock.com, p. 18; Littlekidmoment/Shutterstock.com, p. 19.

For the girls: LKAT, PKAT, and EVAF

Lerner Publications Company
An imprint of Lerner Publishing Group, Inc.
241 First Avenue North
Minneapolis, MN 55401 USA

For reading levels and more information, look up this title at www.lernerbooks.com.

Main body text set in Billy Infant. Typeface provided by SparkyType.

Editor: Alison Lorenz **Photo Editor:** Brianna Kaiser **Lerner team:** Sue Marquis

Library of Congress Cataloging-in-Publication Data

Names: Colella, Jill, author.
Title: Bouncing back with Big Bird : a book about resilience / Jill Colella.
Description: Minneapolis : Lerner Publications, 2021 | Series: Sesame Street character guides | Includes bibliographical references and index. | Audience: Ages 4-8. | Summary: "Big Bird and friends support young readers as they learn how to work through setbacks. Kids learn positive self-talk, how to ask for help, and more so they can tackle any challenge"— Provided by publisher.
Identifiers: LCCN 2020005011 (print) | LCCN 2020005012 (ebook) | ISBN 9781728403908 (library binding) | ISBN 9781728418742 (ebook)
Subjects: LCSH: Resilience (Personality trait) in children—Juvenile literature. | Resilience (Personality trait)—Juvenile literature.
Classification: LCC BF723.R46 C65 2021 (print) | LCC BF723.R46 (ebook) | DDC 154.4/1824—dc23

LC record available at https://lccn.loc.gov/2020005011
LC ebook record available at https://lccn.loc.gov/2020005012

Manufactured in the United States of America
1-48390-48904-5/18/2020